CW01651747

DE:CODE

LEARN THE LANGUAGE OF

CODING

BY WILLIAM ANTHONY

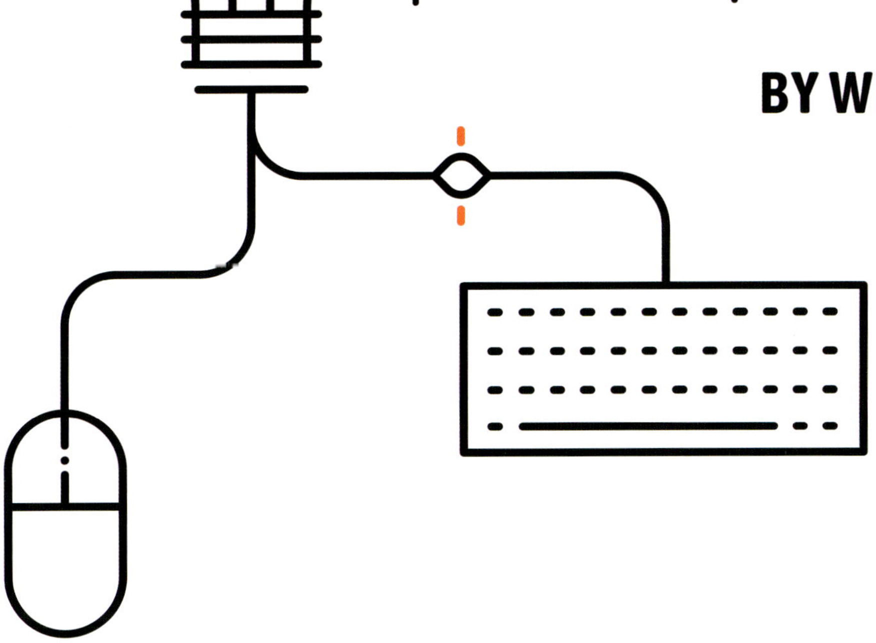

BookLife PUBLISHING

©2019
BookLife Publishing Ltd.
King's Lynn
Norfolk, PE30 4LS

All rights reserved.
Printed in Malaysia.

A catalogue record for this book is available from the British Library.

ISBN: 978-1-78637-693-0

Written by:
William Anthony

Edited by:
Madeline Tyler

Designed by:
Dan Scase

All facts, statistics, web addresses and URLs in this book were verified as valid and accurate at time of writing.

No responsibility for any changes to external websites or references can be accepted by either the author or publisher.

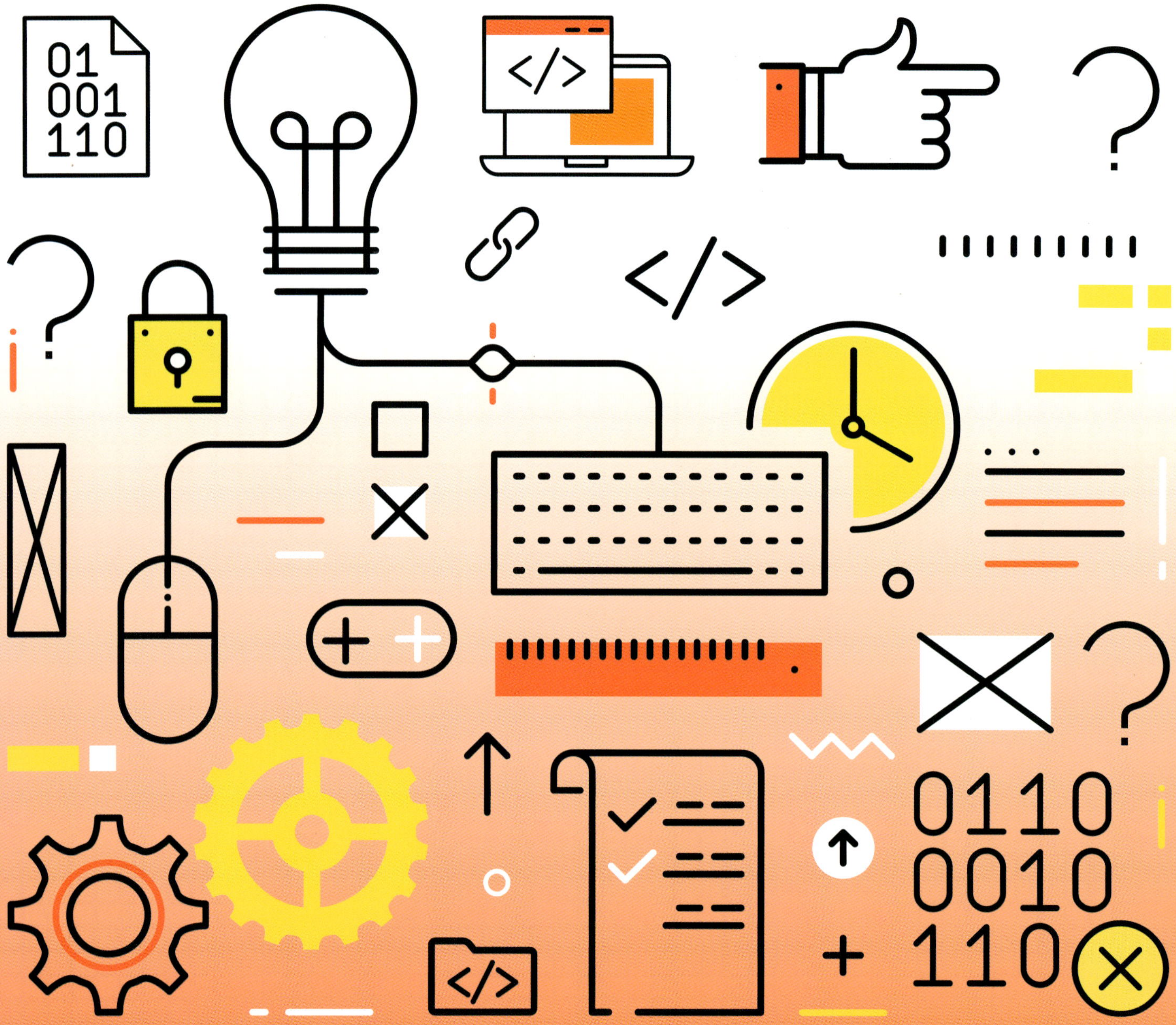

PHOTO CREDITS

All images are courtesy of Shutterstock.com, unless otherwise specified. With thanks to Getty Images, Thinkstock Photo and iStockphoto.
Front Cover – stockchairatgfx, iunewind. 4 – siridhata, Anna Panova, denvitruk. 5 – ksenvitaln, diluck. 6 – Businessvector, pzUH, M-O Vector, ksenvitaln. 7 – Aha-Soft, DG-Studio. 8 – Juli92, Pro Symbols. 9 – AlesiaKan. UfaBizPhoto. 10 – Yakan, Studio Photo MH. 11 – Orkhan Naghiyev, SkillUp. 12 – andromina, 10 FACE. 13 – Giri1992, Boris N. 14 – Gorodenkoff. 15 – ScottMurph, M-O Vector, Irina Sulima. 16 – NeMaria, Thomas Bethge. 17 – Irina Medvedeva Mejg, Aha-Soft, Creative Stall, 300 librarians. 18 – PODIS, lukmanhakim. 19 – Tartila, Arcady. 20 – illustratioz, Vladvm. 21 – Myvector, Nikser. 22 – Myvector, defmorph. 23 – BEST-BACKGROUNDS. 24 – Vdant85, nanovector, Mr.Creative. 25 – ichadsgn, GzP_Design, premium design. 26 – Lidiia, Tetiana Yurchenko, linear_design, sidmay. 27 – Anna Panova, freesoulproduction. 28 – CosmoVector, Yayayoyo. 29 – ZabVector, Telman Bagirov, Shutterstock Vector. 30 – DC Studio. 31 – MapensStudio, Nazarii M, shahsoft.

HOW TO DE:CODE THE LANGUAGE OF CODING

The language of coding can sometimes be difficult to understand, but there's no need to worry. This handy guide will help you learn lots of different words – but first, let's take a look at how to De:Code each of them.

> **BITMAP GRAPHICS**
> **(BIT-MAP GRAH-FIX)**
> *Noun:* drawings created on a computer that are stored as a grid of pixels. See **PIXELS**.

HEADWORD: this shows you how a word is spelt. These words are organised in alphabetical order.

PRONUNCIATION GUIDE: this tells you how to say a word out loud. Say each part exactly how it's written to pronounce the word correctly.

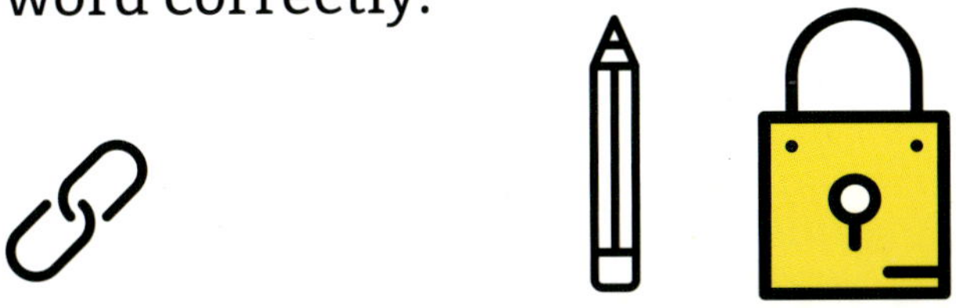

Word class: this is the type of word that the headword is. In this book you will see some of these:

- Noun – a person, place or thing
- Verb – an action word
- Adjective – a describing word

Abbreviations: this is the type of word that the headword is. In this book you will see some of these:

- Initialism – a set of letters taken from several words that are read as individual letters
- Acronym – a set of letters taken from several words that make a new word

Definition: this is what the headword means.

0110
0010
110

RELATED WORDS: this shows you other words that link to the one you're looking at.

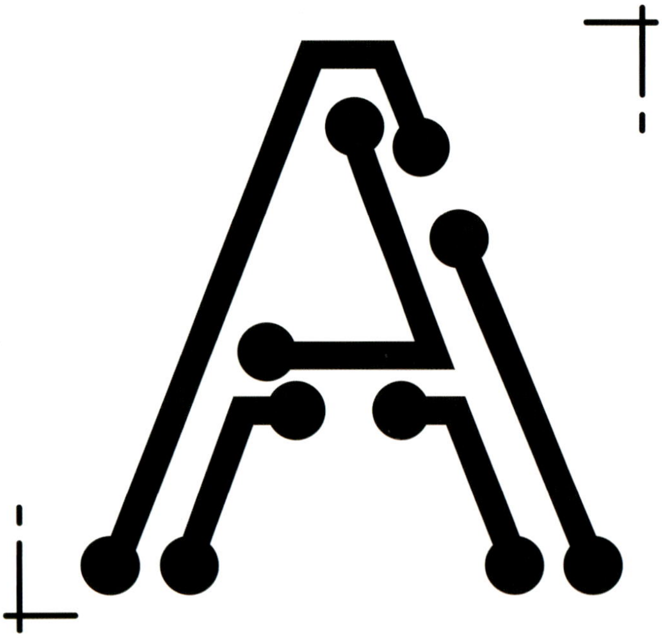

APP

Noun: short for application. An app is a program installed and used on a computer system or portable device. Types of app include games, internet browsers and social media sites.

ARRAY

Noun: a collection of items or values. See **VALUE**.

ASCII (American Standard Code for Information Interchange)

Acronym: a type of code used for storing text code as binary code. See **BINARY**.

AUTOMATED (OR-TUH-MAY-TID)

Adjective: operated automatically by a machine, rather than needing a human.

ABSTRACTION

Noun: the ways a computer hides how complex a piece of software or hardware is by creating a simple user interface to suit the average user. See **USER INTERFACE**.

ALGORITHM

Noun: a set of instructions that a computer follows in the order that they have been given.

ANIMATION

Noun: images that change shape and position very quickly to make it look like they're moving.

BIT

Noun: a binary digit (0 or 1). This is the smallest unit of digital information.

BITMAP GRAPHICS
(BIT-MAP GRAH-FIX)

Noun: drawings created on a computer that are stored as a grid of pixels. See **PIXELS**.

BOOLEAN EXPRESSION
(BOO-LEE-AN EX-PREH-SHUN)

Noun: a logical question that only has two possible answers: TRUE or FALSE. See **LOGIC**.

BOT

Noun: a program that is made to behave like a real person online and can interact with a system or user.

BRANCH

Noun: an instruction in a computer program that can cause a computer to begin a different instruction sequence. See **SEQUENCE**.

BINARY
(BYE-NUH-REE)

Noun: the language that computers use. It is made up of a series of 1s and 0s.

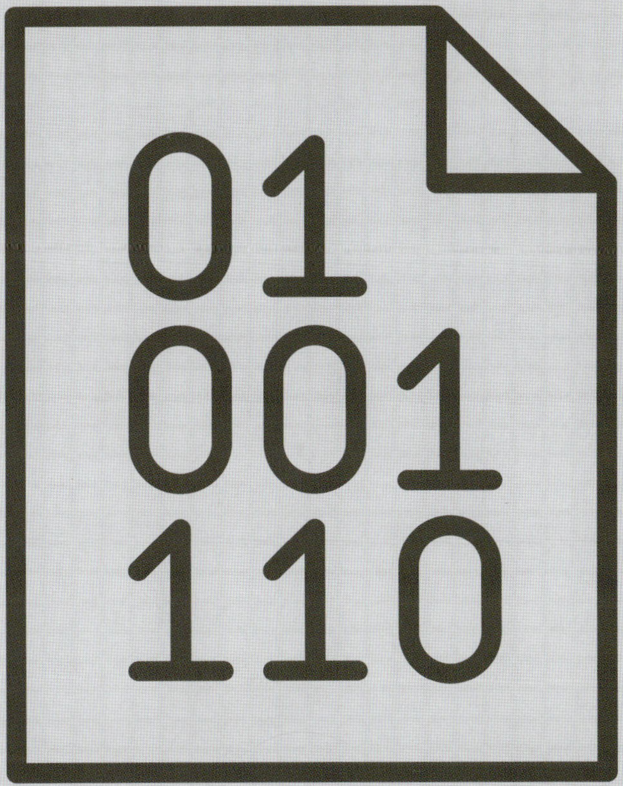

A B C D E F G H I J K L M N O P Q R S T U V W X Y Z

BUG

Noun: an error in a piece of software that stops it from working the way that it should do.

BYTE
(BITE)

Noun: a unit of digital information that contains eight bits, which is stored in a computer. See **BIT**.

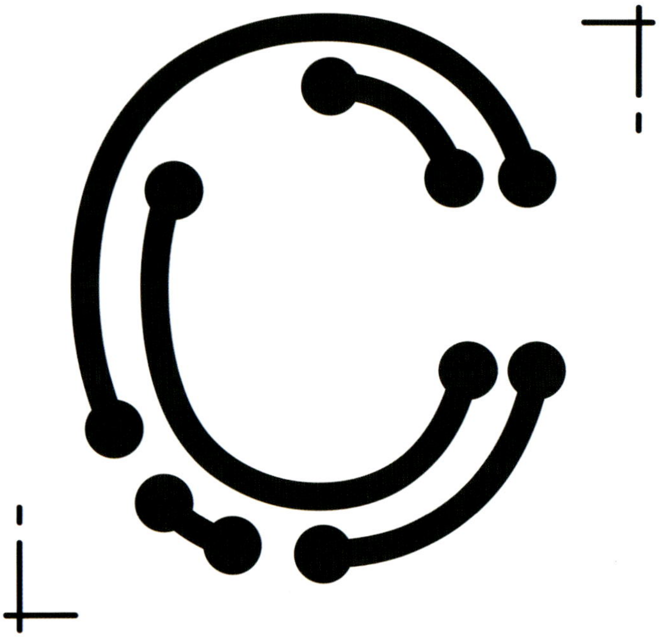

CALL

Verb: to use a function in a program. See **FUNCTION**.

CLONE

Noun: a copy of a sprite or piece of code that can function and run on its own, separate from the original.

CODE

Noun: the language that programmers create and use to tell a computer what to do.

CODING

Verb: putting information and commands into a program to create software, apps and websites.

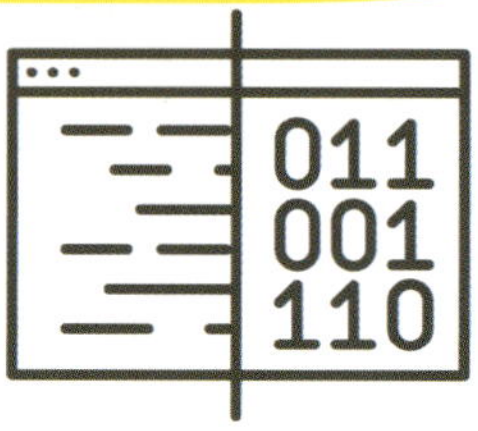

COMPILE

Verb: changing the words used in codes and programs into binary code, which the computer can understand. This can be done by using a compiler. See **BINARY**.

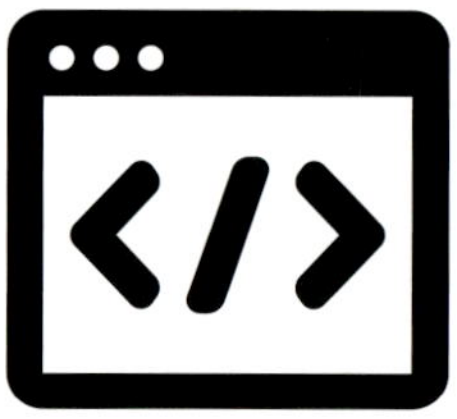

COMPRESSION
(COM-PREH-SHUN)

Noun: a way of making data much smaller so that it takes up less storage memory.

CONDITIONALS
(CON-DIH-SHUN-ALLS)

Noun: statements that only run when certain things happen.

CONTAINER
(CON-TAY-NUR)

Noun: part of a program that can be used to store other items of data.

CSS (Cascading Style Sheets)

Initialism: a set of instructions to describe the formatting (for example, the layout, font and size) of a document, written in a computer language such as HTML. See **HTML**.

COORDINATES
(CO-OR-DIN-UTS)

Noun: two numbers that refer to an exact point on the stage in programming software.
See **STAGE**.

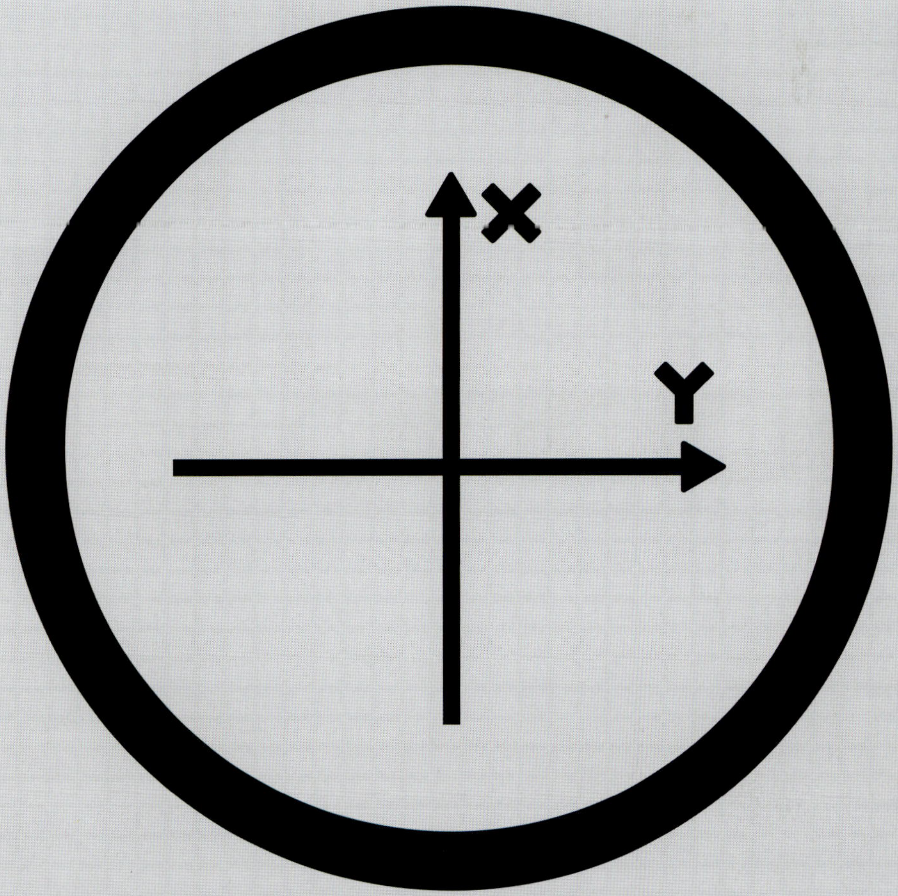

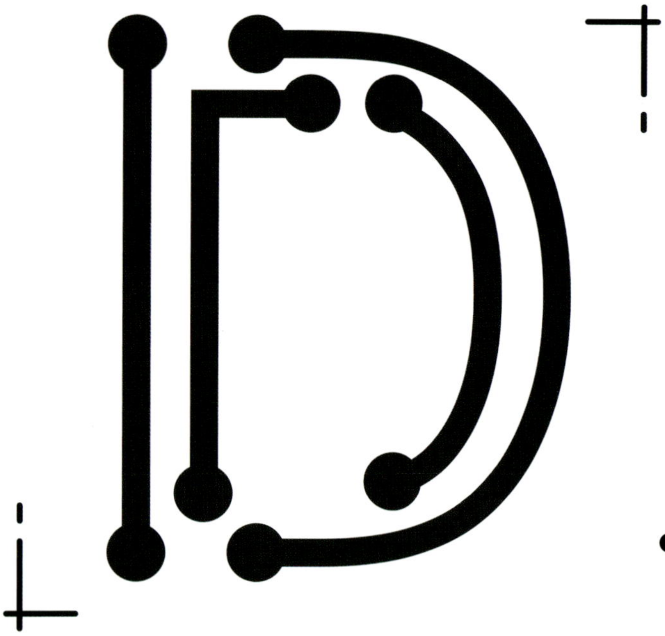

DEBUGGING

Verb: finding and fixing problems in an algorithm or program.

DATA

Noun: information that can be understood by a computer, such as text, images and videos.

DECODE

Verb: to change a coded message into language we can understand. It is also the title of an excellent series of books, one of which you have in your hand!

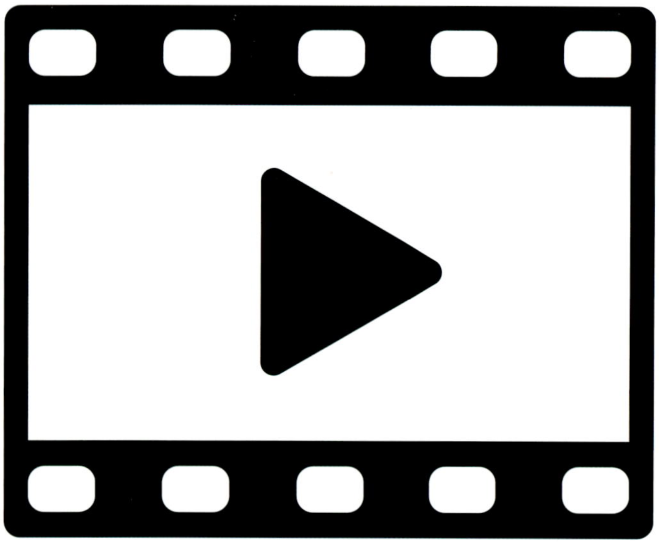

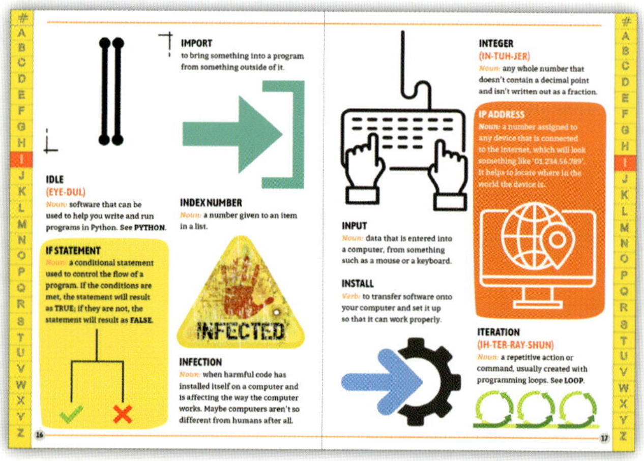

IMPORT
to bring something into a program from something outside of it.

IDLE
(EYE-DUL)
Noun: software that can be used to help you write and run programs in Python. See **PYTHON**.

INDEX NUMBER
Noun: a number given to an item in a list.

IF STATEMENT
Noun: a conditional statement used to control the flow of a program. If the conditions are met, the statement will result as **TRUE**; if they are not, the statement will result as **FALSE**.

INFECTED

INFECTION
Noun: when harmful code has installed itself on a computer and is affecting the way the computer works. Maybe computers aren't so different from humans after all.

16

INPUT
Noun: data that is entered into a computer, from something such as a mouse or a keyboard.

INSTALL
Verb: to transfer software onto your computer and set it up so that it can work properly.

INTEGER
(IN-TUH-JER)
Noun: any whole number that doesn't contain a decimal point and isn't written out as a fraction.

IP ADDRESS
Noun: a number assigned to any device that is connected to the internet, which will look something like '01.234.56.789'. It helps to locate where in the world the device is.

ITERATION
(IH-TER-RAY-SHUN)
Noun: a repetitive action or command, usually created with programming loops. See **LOOP**.

17

DATABASE

Noun: a set of data held in a computer that can be organised and used in lots of different ways. See **DATA**.

DECOMPOSE

Verb: break down a problem or issue with some code into smaller pieces. See **CODE**.

DEVELOPER

Noun: someone who is involved in coding, programming or designing. See **CODING**.

A B C D E F G H I J K L M N O P Q R S T U V W X Y Z

DIGITAL

Adjective: when something uses and stores information as a series of binary 1s and 0s to carry out certain tasks or functions.
See **BINARY**.

DIRECTORY

Noun:
a place where files can be stored in an organised way.

DOWNLOAD

Verb: to copy data from one computer system to another, usually across the internet.

DRIVER

Noun:
a piece of software a computer uses to communicate with hardware such as printers and scanners. There are no cars here.
See **HARDWARE** and **SOFTWARE**.

WORD SEARCH

P	H	A	K	C	R	V	C
Y	D	H	L	O	O	R	N
T	A	P	E	D	A	F	A
H	T	W	Y	E	X	G	C
C	O	D	F	T	J	L	K
H	A	C	K	K	H	O	P
H	F	D	A	T	A	O	Y
L	O	P	E	Z	D	P	N

Can you spot some of the words from this book in a crowd of letters? De:Code this word search and see if you can find every one!

- CODE
- DATA
- HACK
- LOOP
- PYTHON

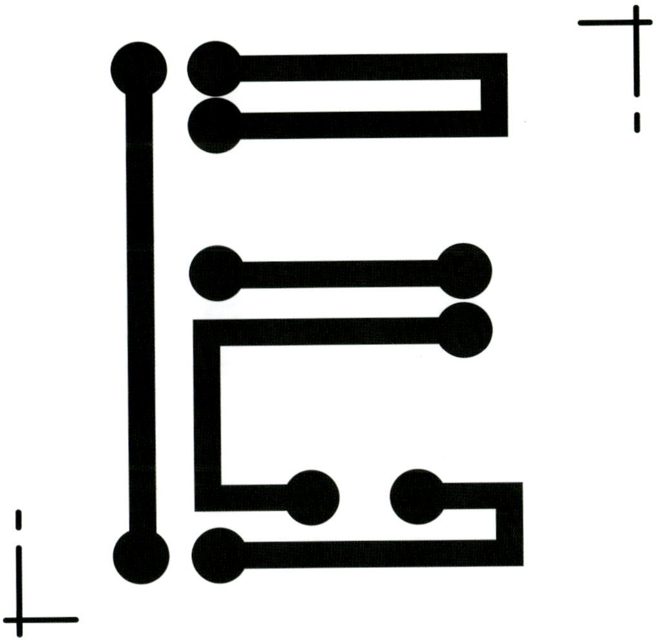

EVENT

Noun: an action that a computer can react to, such as a mouse click.

EXCLUSIVE OR

Noun: an operator written as XOR that results as TRUE when only one of two conditions are true. The conditions can't both be TRUE or both be FALSE. For example, 'person is female' XOR 'person has brown eyes' results in all males with brown eyes and females without brown eyes. See **OPERATOR**.

ELSE STATEMENT

Noun: a way of telling a program to do other actions when an if statement is false. See **IF STATEMENT**.

ENCRYPTION (EN-CRIP-SHUN)

Noun: a way of changing and scrambling information so that it can't be read by anyone who doesn't know the password or key to unscramble it. This makes the information safer.

EXPORT

Verb: send a finished project to the computer to be saved as a file.

ERROR

Noun: a message letting you know that something has gone wrong or is not working as it should. This is often followed with an annoying sound, such as a big 'humph'.

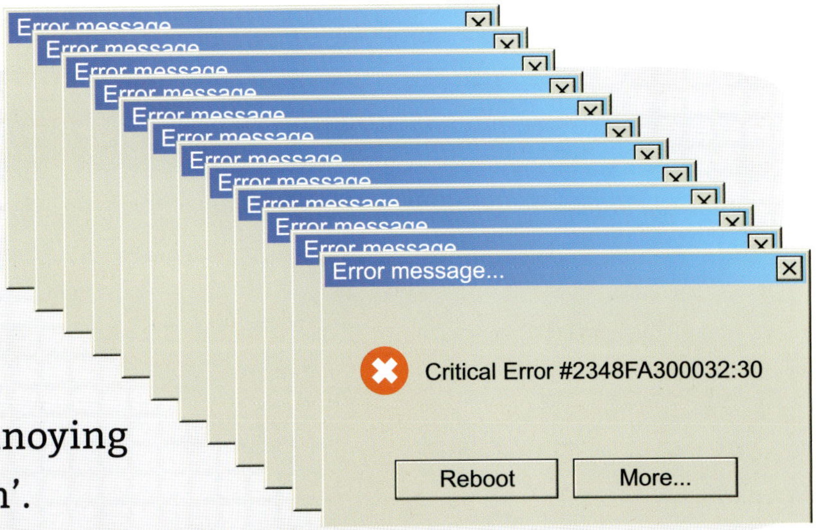

A B C D E F G H I J K L M N O P Q R S T U V W X Y Z

F

FILE NOT FOUND

Noun: a message that means your computer or web browser can't find the file that you've asked it to look for. This is usually a sad time.

FILE

Noun: a collection of data stored in one place under a chosen name.

FLOAT

Noun: a number with a decimal point. The dot in the number 6.2 is a decimal point.

FUNCTION

(FUNK-SHUN)

Noun: a piece of code that helps a larger task to be performed.

WORD JUMBLE

Each group of letters below is a jumbled up word from in this book. Can you rearrange the letters and figure out what each word is? If you're finding it a bit tricky, why not flick through the book to check out some of the words that might be jumbled?

1. AABSEATD
2. BTEY
3. CTHSCAR
4. ORRRE
5. POLO
6. NLOCE
7. SIUVR
8. DRERHWAA

GPU (Graphics Processing Unit)

Initialism: hardware that sends images to the computer screen for the user to see. See **HARDWARE**.

GATE

Noun: something used by computers to make a decision. Gates use input signals to produce output signals based on what a rule tells them to do. See **INPUT** and **OUTPUT**.

GLITCH

Noun: when something does not work correctly, causing a problem.

GLOBAL VARIABLE (GLOW-BUL VAIR-REE-UH-BUL)

Noun: a variable that can be changed and will apply itself to any object or piece of code. See **VARIABLE**.

GRAPHICS (GRAH-FIX)

Noun: visual images and designs that you see on your screen that are not text.

GUI (Graphical User Interface)

Initialism: the things that the user can see and touch or click on. See **USER INTERFACE**.

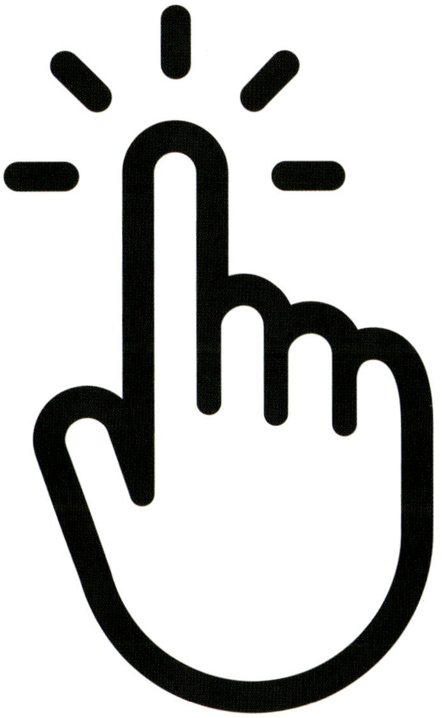

ANSWERS:
1. DATABASE 2. BYTE 3. SCRATCH
4. ERROR 5. LOOP 6. CLONE 7. VIRUS 8. HARDWARE

H

HACK

Verb: to break into a computer system to find problems with the code, or to cause harm to the computer. See **CODE**.

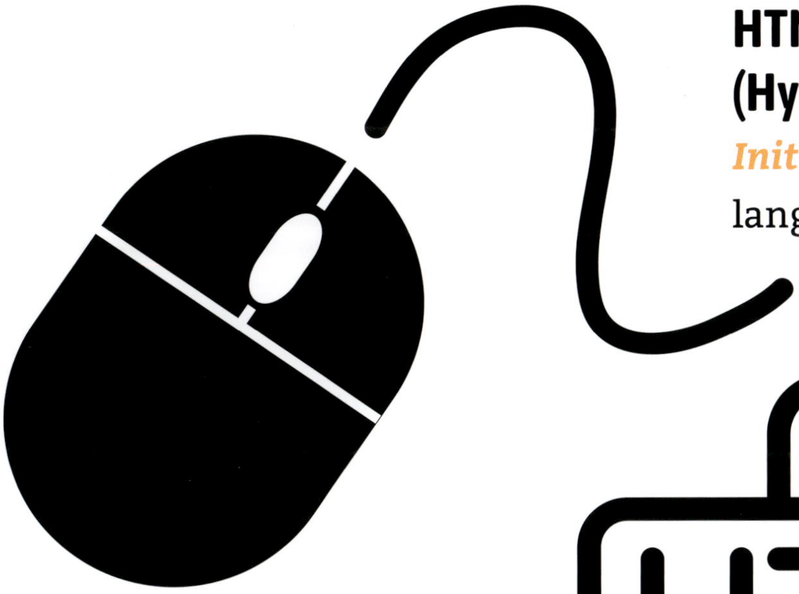

HTML
(Hypertext Markup Language)

Initialism: one of the first coding languages designed to be used for formatting web pages.

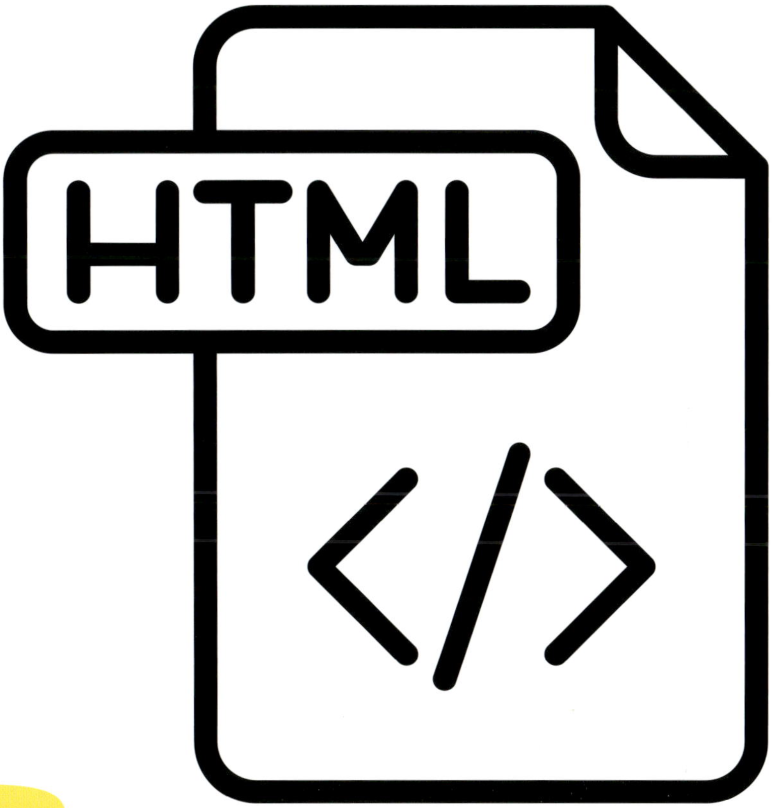

HARDWARE

Noun: the physical parts of a computer, such as the mouse and keyboard.

HEIGHT

Noun: how tall an image or interactive object is.

HEX COLOUR

Noun: a system for choosing specific colours by using a hexadecimal code. For example, the code for this yellow background is #fddc04.
See **HEXADECIMAL**.

HTTP
(Hypertext Transfer Protocol)

Initialism: a set of rules for transferring files and messages on the World Wide Web.
See **WORLD WIDE WEB**.

HEXADECIMAL
(HEX-UH-DESS-IH-MUL)

Noun: a number system based around the number 16, where 0–9 are represented as 0–9, and 10–15 are represented as A to F.

A B C D E F G H I J K L M N O P Q R S T U V W X Y Z

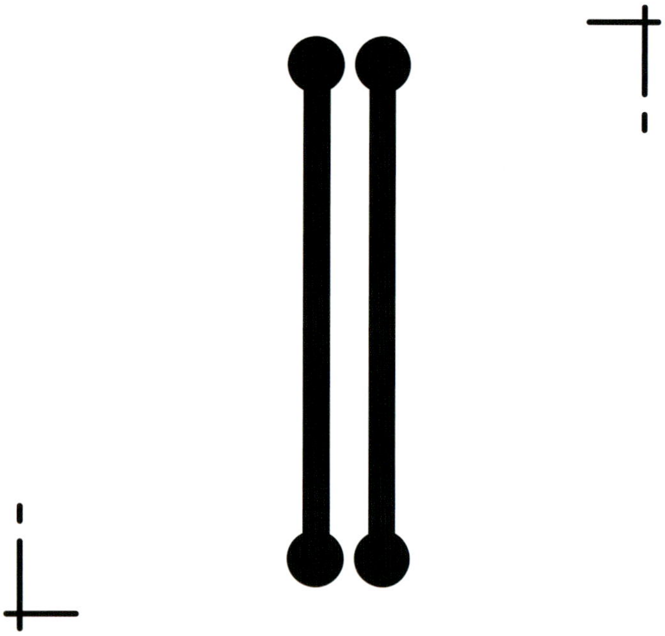

IDLE

(EYE-DUL)

Noun: software that can be used to help you write and run programs in Python. See **PYTHON**.

IF STATEMENT

Noun: a conditional statement used to control the flow of a program. If the conditions are met, the statement will result as TRUE; if they are not, the statement will result as FALSE. See **CONDITIONALS** and **PROGRAM**.

IMPORT

Verb: to bring something into a program from something outside it. See **PROGRAM**.

INDEX NUMBER

Noun: a number given to an item in a list.

INFECTION

Noun: when harmful code has installed itself on a computer and is affecting the way the computer works. Maybe computers aren't so different from humans after all.

INPUT

Noun: data that is entered into a computer from hardware such as a mouse or a keyboard. See **HARDWARE**.

INSTALL

Verb: to transfer software onto your computer and set it up so that it can work properly. See **SOFTWARE**.

INTEGER

(IN-TUH-JER)

Noun: any whole number that doesn't contain a decimal point and isn't written out as a fraction.

IP ADDRESS

Noun: a number assigned to any device that is connected to the internet, which will look something like '01.234.56.789'. It helps to locate where in the world the device is.

ITERATION

(IH-TER-RAY-SHUN)

Noun: a repetitive action or command, usually created with programming loops. See **LOOP**.

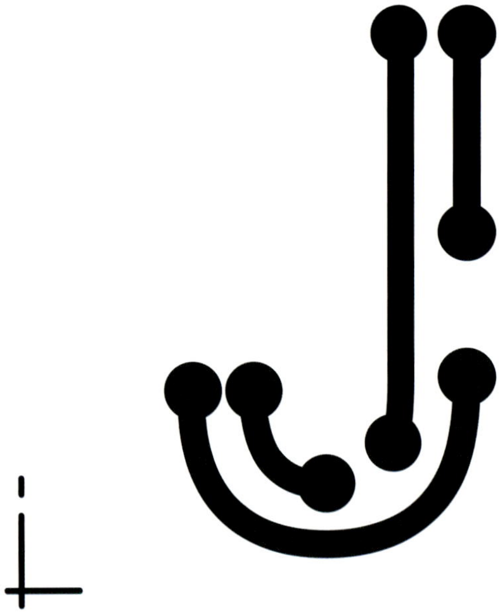

JAVASCRIPT

Noun: a high-level programming language used to code computers. See **CODING**.

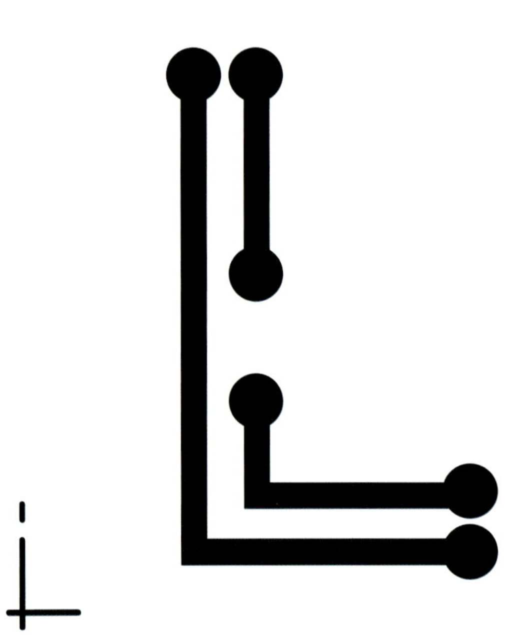

LOCAL VARIABLE
(LOW-KUL VAIR-REE-UH-BUL)

Noun: a variable that can be changed and applied to a single object or piece of code. The variable won't apply itself to clones. See **CLONE**, **CODE** and **VARIABLE**.

LOGIC
(LOH-JIK)

Noun: the decision-making process used in programming and when writing algorithms. See **ALGORITHM**.

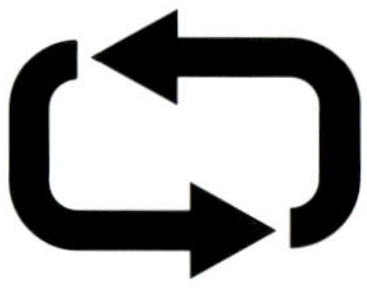

LOOP

Noun: part of a program that repeats itself over and over again, to stop the need for code being typed out lots of times.

LIBRARY

Noun: a selection of functions stored in one place that can be used in lots of different projects. See **FUNCTION**.

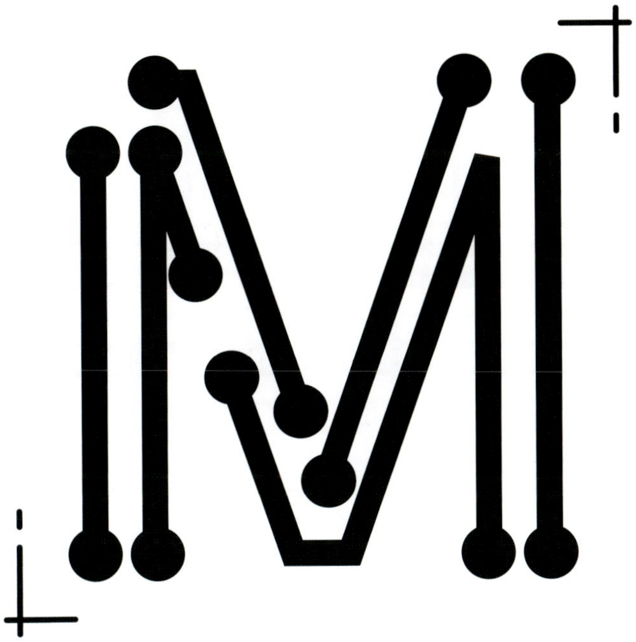

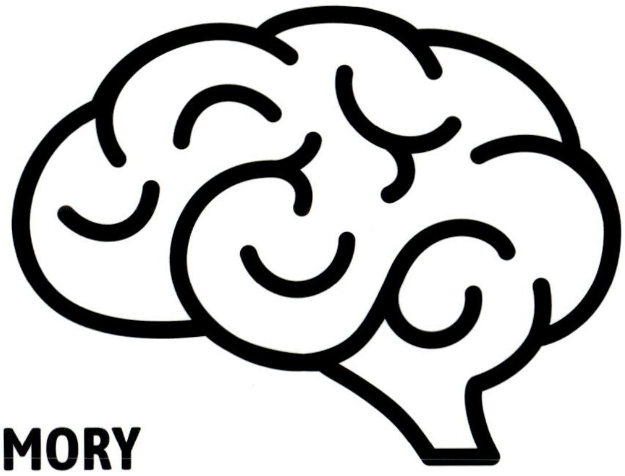

MEMORY

Noun: a computer chip that stores and remembers data. Luckily, computers don't forget things like humans do!

MACHINE CODE

Noun: the basic language that a computer understands.

MESSAGE

Noun: information that can be sent between two or more sprites in Scratch. See **SCRATCH** and **SPRITE**.

MACRO

Noun: a computer script that will record a chain of actions and repeat them for you.

MALWARE

Noun: harmful software designed to mess with the normal operation of a computer. See **SOFTWARE**.

MODULE

(MOH-DUEL)

Noun: a section of code that performs part of a program. See **CODE** and **PROGRAM**.

MORPH

(MORF)

Verb: to smoothly change one graphic or element into another.

OPERATING SYSTEM

Noun: the main program in a computer that controls the way the device works and makes it possible for other programs to function.

NETWORK

Noun: computers and devices within a building or area that are linked together.

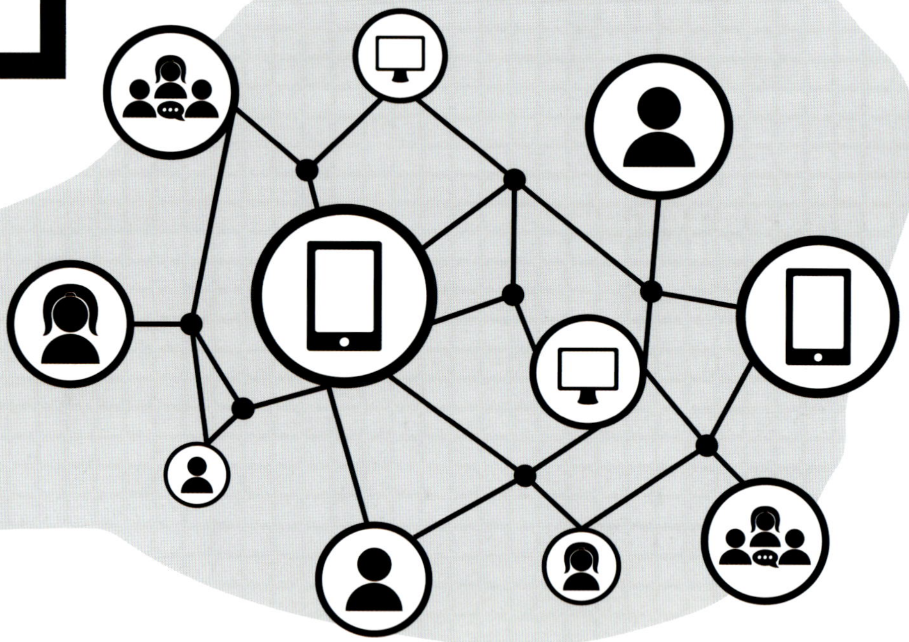

NULL

Adjective: empty and without a value. See **VALUE**.

OPERATOR

Noun: a symbol that represents an action or a process. Some operators are used for mathematics, such as + or – for adding and subtracting. Others, such as Boolean operators, work with TRUE and FALSE values. See **BOOLEAN EXPRESSION**.

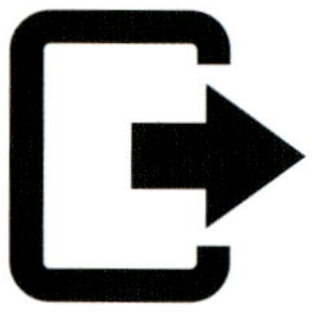

OUTPUT

Noun: data produced by a program that can be seen by the user.

PARAMETER
(PUH-RAH-MIH-TUR)

Noun: an extra piece of information passed to a function to customise it for a specific need. See **FUNCTION**.

PATCH

Noun: a type of update sent out by developers to improve or fix problems in software that has already been released.

PATTERN MATCHING

Verb: attempting to match values against patterns and, if wanted, attaching variables to the matches. See **VALUE** and **VARIABLE.**

PERL

Noun: a complicated but popular software programming language, which is used widely on the internet.

PHYSICS
(FIZ-IKS)

Noun: the science behind how different things move and affect each other. When coding things like games that simulate real life, it is important to get the physics correct to recreate things like gravity.

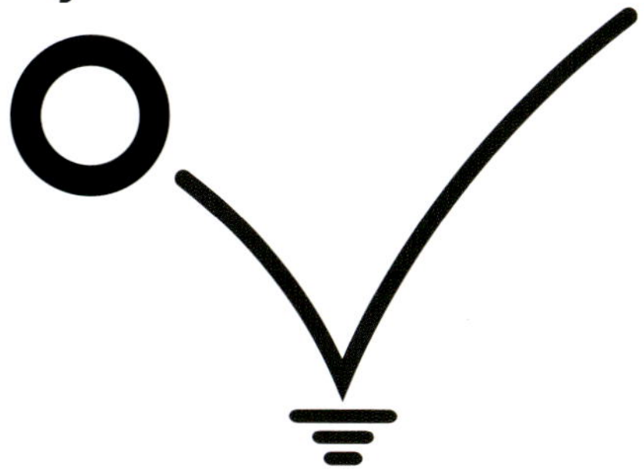

PIXELS

Noun: the tiny units of a digital image. When you look at a picture on a screen, you are looking at a collection of hundreds, thousands or even hundreds of thousands of tiny coloured dots.

PLUG-IN

Noun: an extra bit of software code, such as Flash, that needs to be added to your browser before you can view or use certain types of content.

PORT

Noun: numbers used by a computer to create an address for a program. See **PROGRAM**.

PROCESSOR

Noun: the computer chip inside a computer that is used to run programs.

PROGRAM

Noun: a collection of instructions or algorithms designed to make processes simple. See **ALOGORITHM**.

PROJECT

Noun: a file that includes all the sprites, scripts, sounds and backgrounds that you might be working on. See **FILE** and **SPRITE.**

PROTOTYPE

Noun: a trial model built to test how well an idea, process or piece of code works before developing it further. See **CODE**.

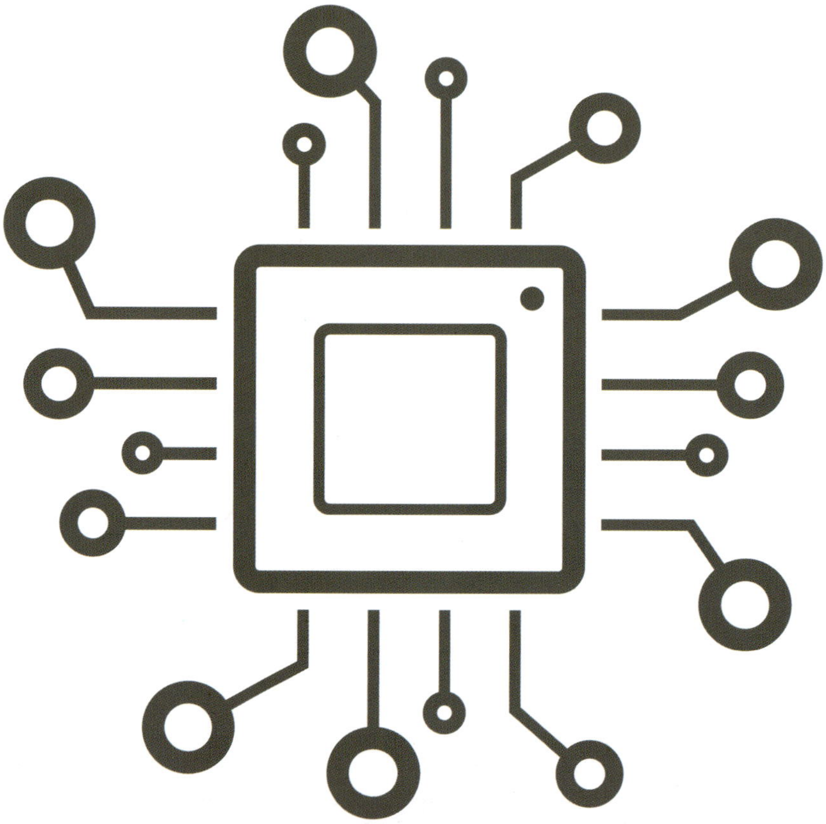

PYTHON

Noun: a programming language based on using only text. Don't worry, it's not a snake.

A B C D E F G H I J K L M N O P Q R S T U V W X Y Z

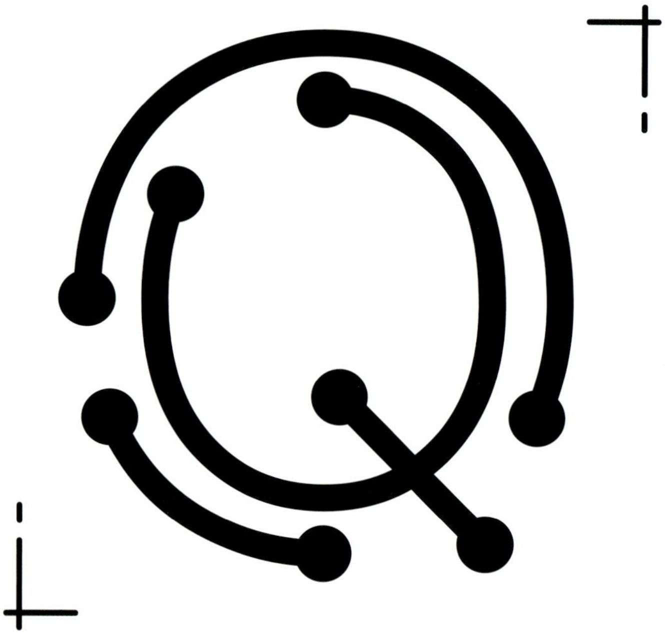

QR CODE

Noun: a square with lots of smaller square and rectangular shapes inside that can be scanned by a device and used to launch a website.

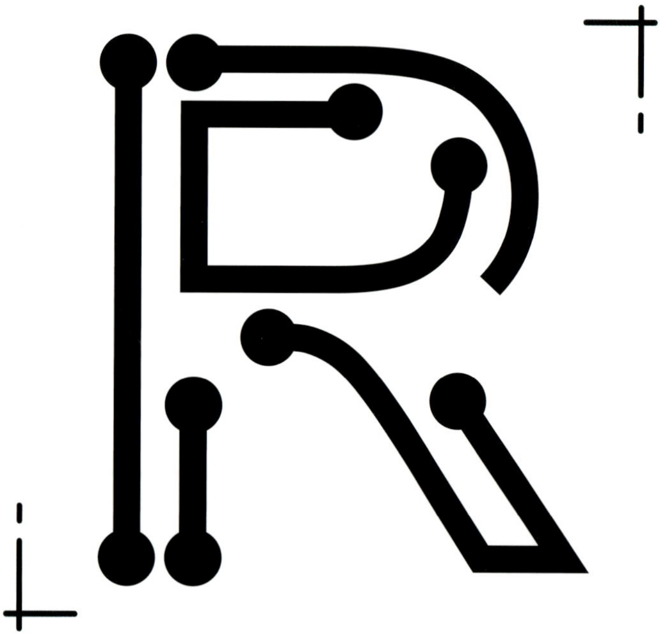

RANDOM

Noun: a programming function that allows and creates constantly changing outcomes. Video games use this lot. See **FUNCTION**.

RECURSION (RE-KUR-ZHUN)

Noun: when a function calls itself. See **CALL** and **FUNCTION**.

REPETITION

Noun: when part of a program repeats itself by using a repeat statement or loop. For example, in animation you may repeat the movements of a character to make it look like it's moving along. See **ANIMATION** and **LOOP.**

RUN

Verb: start the program!

RUNTIME

Noun: the length of time that a program is running for.

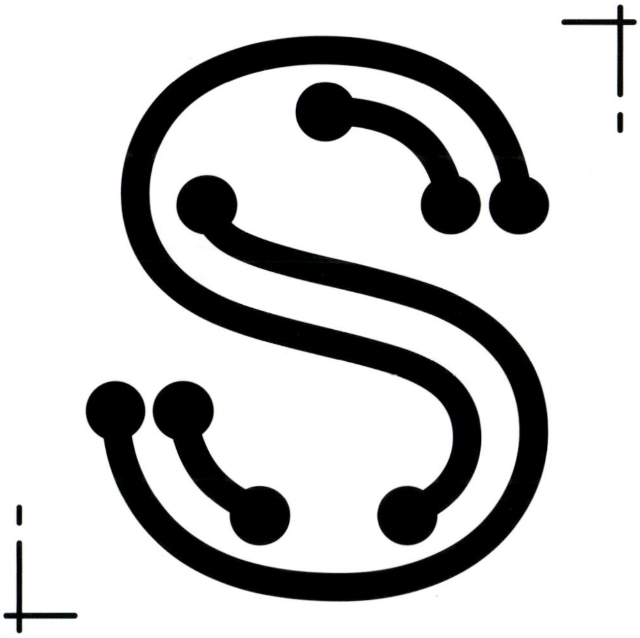

SEARCH ENGINE

Noun: a program that searches for items that include chosen keywords or characters in a database.

SCALE

Verb: to set the size or zoom of an item.

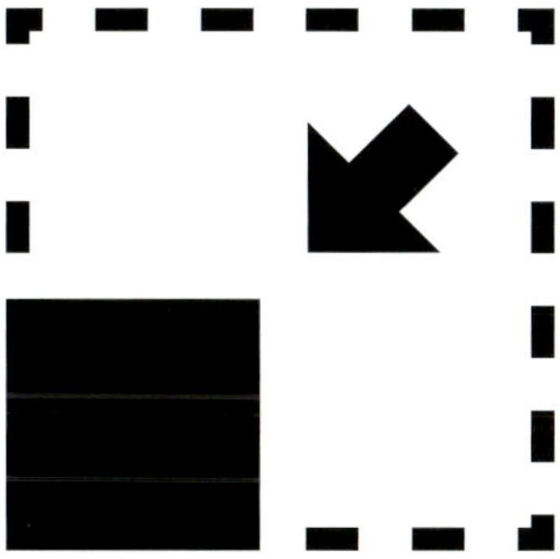

SCRATCH

Noun: a visual programming language that makes it easy to code programs. See **CODING** and **PROGRAM**.

SEQUENCE

(SEE-KWENSE)

Noun: a set of instructions or actions that are carried out in the same order every time, which control what happens in a computer. See **STATEMENT**.

SERVER

Noun: a computer used for storing files that can be accessed by the network. See **NETWORK**.

DID YOU KNOW?

A programming language is a set of commands, instructions and other pieces of code that are used to create software. Visual programming language is the same but uses images rather than text.

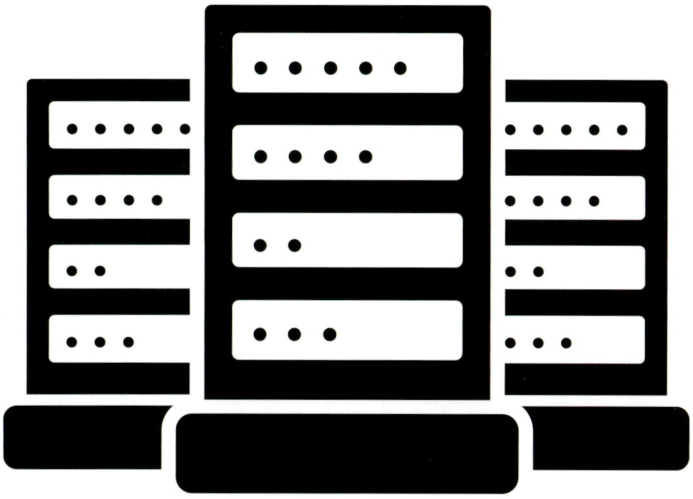

SIMULATION
(SIM-YOU-LAY-SHUN)

Noun: a computer-based recreation of something that happens or exists in real life.

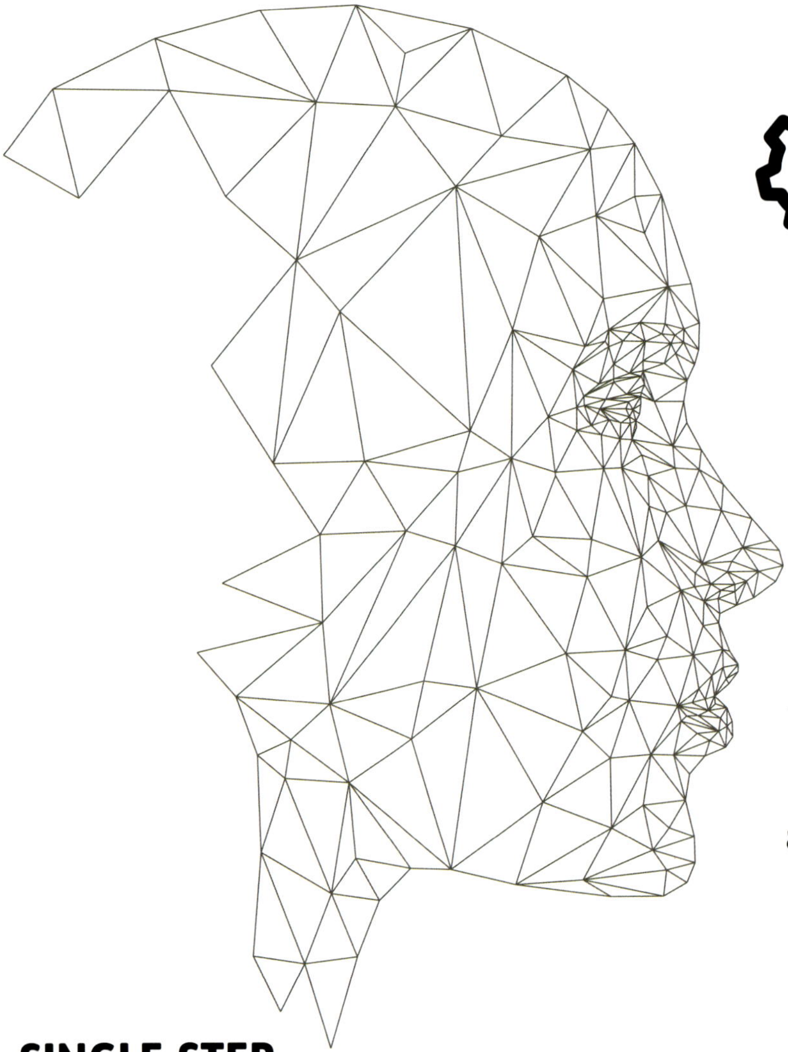

SOFTWARE

Noun: programs that run on a computer and control how it works.

SOURCE CODE

Noun: code viewed in its most basic format without being processed by a computer. It is also known as raw code. See **CODE**.

SINGLE-STEP

Noun: a method of making programs run just one step at a time.

SOCKET

Noun: the combination of a port and an IP address, which allows programs to send data to each other over the internet. See **IP ADDRESS** and **PORT**.

A B C D E F G H I J K L M N O P Q R S T U V W X Y Z

SPRITE

Noun: a bitmap graphic that you can move or animate using code. See **BITMAP GRAPHICS.**

STAGE

Noun: the screen area of Scratch in which you can watch projects run. See **SCRATCH.**

STATEMENT

Noun: the smallest complete instruction that programming language can be broken down into.

STRING

Noun: a series of characters, such as letters, numbers or symbols. Not the material that cats play with.

SYNTAX (SIN-TAX)

Noun: rules that decide how a program must be put together before it can work properly. See **PROGRAM.**

A B C D E F G H I J K L M N O P Q R S T U V W X Y Z

T

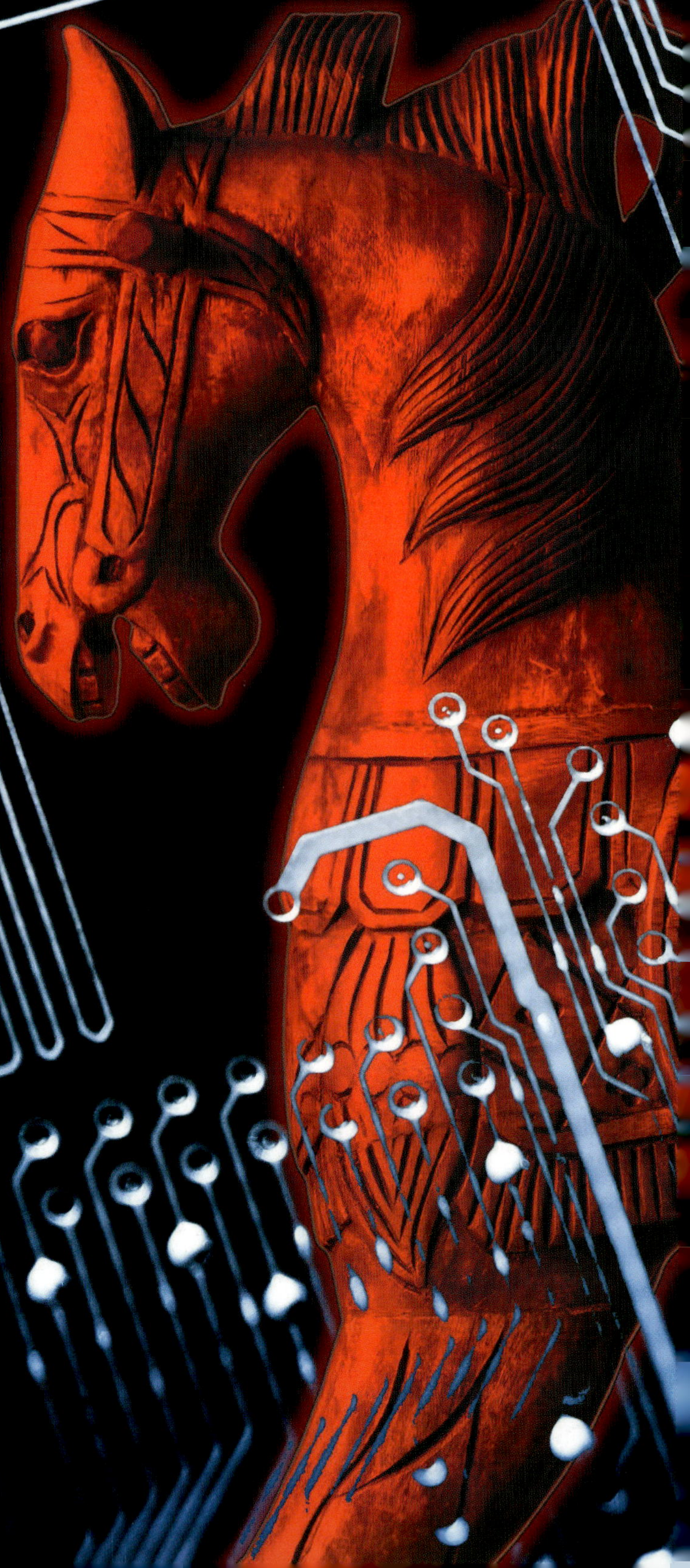

TROJAN

Noun: a program that appears harmless but is carrying viruses or even other programs within it that will damage a computer or allow someone to hack into it. See **HACK**.

DID YOU KNOW?

The word 'trojan' comes from an ancient story. In order to invade the city of Troy, the ancient Greeks made the Trojans a huge wooden horse as a peace offering to end the war. The Trojans took the offering inside their city gates, but it was a trick! Greek warriors were hidden inside and, that night, they climbed out and opened the gates to Troy for the Greeks to invade.

TWEAK
Verb: to change a very small part of something to make it work slightly better or differently. This is usually done during the final stages of completing a project.

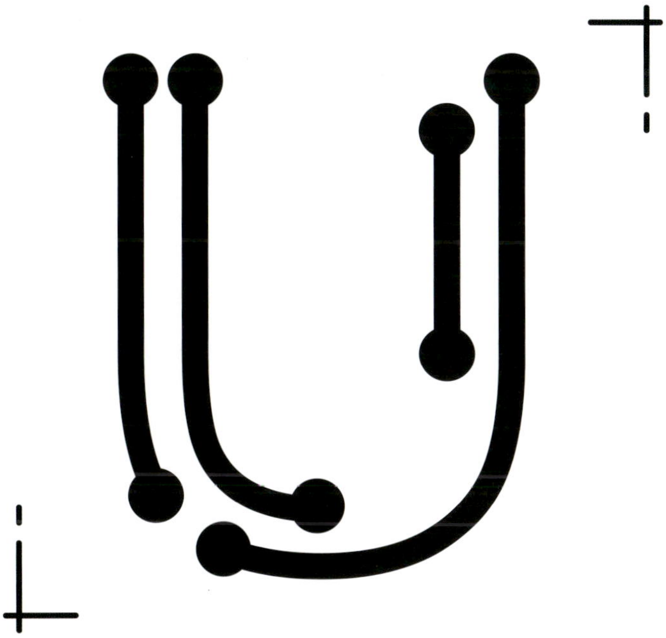

USB (Universal Serial Bus)
Initialism: a system for connecting a device to a computer.

USER-FRIENDLY
Adjective: a type of program that is built in an easy-to-use way.

UNICODE
Noun: a digital code for computers that lets them show text in different languages.
See **CODE**.

URL (Uniform Resource Locator)
Initialism: a website address.

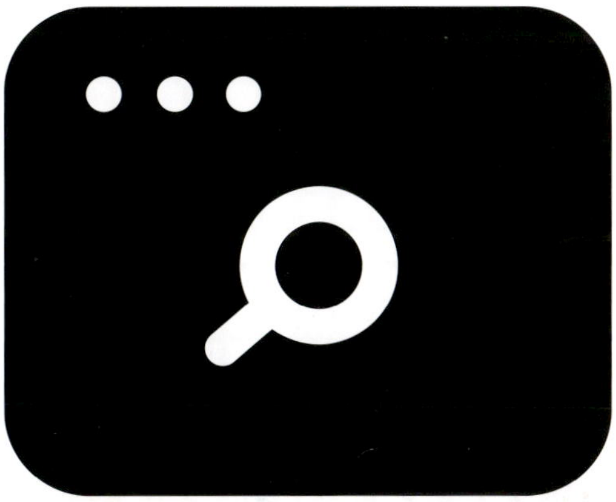

USER INTERFACE
Noun: the way a user can interact with a computer, and the options they are given to do so.

V

VARIABLE
(VAIR-REE-UH-BUL)

Noun: a value that can change depending on information given to a program. See **VALUE**.

VERSION

Noun: a form of a product that is different from other forms of the same product.

VALUE

Noun: the content of a field or variable, which could be lettered or numbered data. See **VARIABLE**.

VIRUS

Noun: a type of malware that multiplies to spread across multiple computers and affects how they perform. See **MALWARE**.

WORD RUSH

There are a lot of words in this book, but how many of them can you make from these letters in just 2 minutes? You can use each letter square just once for each word. Play on your own or grab a friend to challenge. Find a pen, get some paper and start the timer! 3... 2... 1...

W	T	D	G	U	I
F	D	M	L	O	P
A	E	R	T	F	C
L	K	A	U	H	B
E	A	I	N	G	U
S	M	P	O	D	K

W

Z

WHILE LOOP

Noun: a loop that continues to repeat while a condition is true.

WIDTH

Noun: how wide an image or interactive object is.

WORLD WIDE WEB

Noun: a collection of web pages found on the internet.

ZERO-DAY PATCH

Noun: an update for a piece of software set to be sent out on the day of release. See **PATCH**.

ZIP

Noun: a file that has been compressed to hold lots of information without taking up lots of storage. ZIP files are much easier to transfer over websites than larger folders. See **COMPRESSION**.

CROSSWORD

There are lots of definitions to learn in this book, so how well do you think you know them? Use the definitions below to work out which words fit into the boxes on the grid!

ACROSS:

3. when something does not work correctly, causing a problem
6. finding and fixing problems in an algorithm or program
9. data produced by a program that can be seen by the user
10. someone who is involved in coding, programming or designing
11. programs that run on a computer and control how it works
12. the computer chip inside a computer that is used to run programs
14. the language that computers use, which is made up of a series of 1s and 0s
15. an action that a computer can react to, such as a mouse click

DOWN:

1. a type of malware that multiplies to spread across multiple computers and affects how they perform
2. how wide an image or interactive object is
4. to bring something into a program from something outside it
5. a place where you can store files in an organised way
7. a program installed and used on a computer system or portable device
8. hardware that sends images to the computer screen for the user to see
11. a computer used for storing files that can be accessed by the network
13. the screen area of Scratch in which you can watch projects run

ANSWERS: 1. VIRUS, 2. WIDTH, 3. GLITCH, 4. IMPORT, 5. DIRECTORY, 6. DEBUGGING, 7. APP, 8. GPU , 9. OUTPUT, 10. DEVELOPER, 11(A). SOFTWARE, 11(D). SERVER, 12. PROCESSOR, 13. STAGE, 14. BINARY, 15. EVENT